Anthony Siracusa, Ph.D
Randall Fisher, LICSW

Your Psychotherapy and Counseling Companion

Your Psychotherapy and Counseling Companion
Subtitle

v5.0

Outskirts Press, Inc.
http://www.outskirtspress.com

ISBN: 978-1-4787-3906-7

PRINTED IN THE UNITED STATES OF AMERICA

Dedications

For Maggie

For Jacob, Talia, and Jai

To all those hoping to find their way…My patients, past and present

And

To all the family and friends I love!

AJS, 2015

For Cory

Teresa, Grace, Noah and Alexandra

To Corey, Jaimey, Joel, Sawyer and Seth

To all my past and present patients who have so graciously inspired me, especially MP

RDF, 2015

Table of Contents

The only person educated is the one who
has learned how to learn and change.

—*Carl Rogers*

I. INTRODUCTION

For the past 30 years we have dedicated our professional lives to helping people like you cope with the personal and relational problems of life. These problems have included issues of low self-esteem and coping with the stress of daily life. Moreover, we frequently deal with grief from the loss of a significant relationship or difficulties with anxiety and depression.On occasion we work with people with deep, debilitating psychological problems. Our work has been to help clients discover for themselves the most effective and efficient way to bring positive change to their lives. This partnership, between therapist and client, to develop strategies and courses of action, is at the heart of helping people change.

That partnership inspired our commitment and desire to help clients create a plan of action on how to best achieve their goals. Our curiosity on how to best help our clients change their lives resulted in us continuously searching for methods and strategies to help people, just like you, use their psychotherapy and counseling more effectively and efficiently. While people may face life barriers in trying to create personal change, one over riding challenge stands out. A client or patient must decide how to best incorporate into their daily life the methods and/or strategies developed in their therapy session. We believe this to be central to the change process in psychotherapy.

As we have often noted with our clients, there are 168 hours in a week. Assuming a person sleeps for 56 hours (most people probably sleep less these days), that leaves 112 hours of waking time. If a person goes to therapy 1 hour a week, that leaves 111 hours when he or she is back into the routines, demands and stress of work, school, caretaking, parenting, family, etc. Because of that reality, the question becomes, how can we best use that 1 hour of therapy to bring about the change you desire? Our intention in developing ***Your Psychotherapy and Counseling Companion,*** is to help you and your therapist make your 1 hour of therapy more effective and bring the life changes you desire more quickly.

As we have sought to help clients increase the benefit from their therapy, several important questions have emerged:

- What is the best way to increase the effectiveness and probable use of the ideas from a therapy session?
- Are there specific strategies that can support "the work" of therapy?
- What are the most effective strategies to help clients use the experience of psychotherapy in their daily life?
- Is there a way to make the relationship with your therapist more effective?

Over the years we have tried a variety approaches to answer those questions. At various times we have used workbooks, CDs, articles, tapes, etc., with our clients. And while each of those strategies provided some benefit, none quite measured up to exactly what we were trying to do. Over time, we came to believe that a more flexible, personal and individually tailored tool was needed.

Extensive feedback from thousands of clients provided clues that eventually led to an important discovery. It became very clear that when our clients had a concrete portable record of their therapy that they could use **between** sessions, the speed of personal change greatly accelerated. After several years of real-life testing, refinement and, above all, input from our clients, we developed ***Your Psychotherapy and Counseling Companion***. We think you will find **"The Companion"** easy to use, helpful and interesting. It will become your personal record that travels with you on your personal journey of change.

II. Overview

We created ***Your Psychotherapy and Counseling Companion*** to help people have a more efficient and useful psychotherapy experience. We think of the book as a tool whose purpose is to be an **assistant** and **support** to you while you are engaged in therapy. We have structured **"The Companion"** with two essential goals in mind. One was to give you a brief overview of what to expect from your therapy experience. In a sense, we have spent some time to prepare you for the experience of being "in therapy." To that end, we discuss some basic elements of the therapy process. Our second goal in writing the book, was to create a tool that would be a concrete support to you while you are attending therapy. That support is found in the use of "session outline" sheets. These sheets, completed at the end of the session with the help of the therapist, create a portable ongoing reference of your work. The outline sheets are designed using a structured format to guide you in recording essential information from each session. This information is critical to your success. Having a written documentation of each session available to you at any time is an enormous advantage. We fully appreciate, as do most therapists, the effort and commitment of time, energy and money you have made to change your life. **"The Psychotherapy Companion"** has been developed to maximize your opportunity for success. A successful psychotherapy experience will likely mean that your emotional and personal life have changed for the better and the goals you had for yourself when you started therapy have been largely achieved. So more precisely, what is the mission of **"Your Psychotherapy Companion"** and how is it used?

To realize "Your Companion's" primary goal, we have structured the book to solve and address a crucial barrier to successful therapy. That barrier is how to "bridge and connect" what is learned, discovered or recommended from a therapy session to your larger life. You will quickly discover that using "Your Psychotherapy and Counseling Companion" builds and connects parts of you, and parts of your life that, when brought together, begins to lower stress and sadness. **"The Companion"** is the material to build your own bridge. **"The Companion"** will travel with you from session to session and session to life. And as you use that bridge session after session, you will be creating the change you are seeking. Second, the written format also creates a permanent chronicle of your work in therapy. This chronicle will describe session by session **what** you accomplished and **how** it was done. In a true sense, **"The Companion"** will become your own personal historical reference book of change.

A final note: You will notice we use the term "psychotherapy" to include the activity of counseling. This is simply done to make for an easier read. Psychotherapy and counseling are slightly different, and the difference is explained later in the narrative.

How "The Psychotherapy Companion" Is Organized

"The Companion" is organized into three parts that reflect and describe aspects of the psychotherapy process or flow. The first part of **"The Companion"** offers some background information on the psychotherapy experience and gives several examples of activity and processes common to psychotherapy and counseling. We also give brief explanations, reasons and purposes for the use of the activities. For example, in this part of the book, there are sections on emotional intelligence, medication and some examples of psychotherapy "homework." These sections are brief but provide a useful start to begin understanding and preparing for your therapy. Second, the book provides a general description of the "flow" of the therapy process. This flow is broken into three phases: beginning, middle and ending. These beginning, middle and ending phases of psychotherapy and counseling, provide a core element for **"The Companion."** For each phase there are individual session sheets provided to document insights, discoveries and recommendations from each clinical encounter. You will find the outline page will have different questions and headings depending upon which phase of therapy you are working in. Not surprisingly, the middle, or ongoing, phase usually requires the most sessions because this is where most of "the work of therapy" is completed. Third, each session, whether the first, the ongoing or ending, will use a structured format to focus on the key considerations and parts of each particular session. These key considerations are generally seen as crucial aspects of a particular phase or session.

At this point, it might be useful to quickly look at these session outlines to get a sense of their focus. It is also important to remember that it is impossible to correctly predict how many sessions it will take to complete a particular phase. Though we have included only one session page for the initial or ending phase, in fact, these phases may take more than one session.

"The Companion" uses several tried-and-tested ideas to help you in your therapy process. For example, **"Your Psychotherapy and Counseling Comapnion"** is designed to give you a strucured weekly session sheet for each of your sessions. This structured, individualized approach helps to make information more easily organized and understood. Though **"The Companion"** is structured and highly organized, you will find it to be flexible, personal and highly adaptive to your needs. This personalized and flexible approach is one of the big differences between **"The Companion"** and workbooks or curriculums. **"The Companion's"** standardized, flexible format helps you, and your therapist, organize information and strategies specific to your therapy session. This approach helps you to focus your therapy and avoid therapy "drift." **"The Companion"** strikes a balance between structure, which helps keep the psychotherapy focused on goals and objectives: and flexibility: which ensures that your individualized needs are being addressed.

"We can't change the past,

so we change how people are thinking,

feeling and behaving today.

—Albert Ellis

III. Common Characteristics of the Psychotherapy Experience

A. The Three Phases of Treatment

The **beginning** or the **first** phase of treatment is used to accomplish, at least, two important purposes. One purpose is to identify why you are seeking therapy. What problems or issues are you seeking help with? What goals do you have? What are you hoping to accomplish or change in your life? If your life gets better how will it be different? A very common task in the beginning phase is for you and your therapist to try to identify a recent "event" that might have motivated you to seek out therapy. This event is often called the precipitating event. The beginning phase is also crucial to establishing the therapeutic contract or relationship.

The **ongoing** phase of therapy focuses on the issues and goals identified in the beginning phase. To a large extent, this phase is dedicated to clarifying problems and developing interventions. The **ending** phase reviews the progress made toward resolving personal difficulties you articulated in the beginning phase. It is also a time for you to provide feedback to your therapist concerning your work with him or her. And finally, the ending phase can be used to discuss your overall experience with psychotherapy.

B. The Therapeutic Relationship: Fit, Contract/Alliance, Intervention and Ending Psychotherapy

There is much research and psychological study that suggests the therapeutic relationship is one of the most important aspects of successful therapy, if not "the" most important.

What is the therapeutic relationship, and how is it different from other relationships in life? First, it is very important to remember the therapeutic relationship is a professional relationship. First and foremost, it means that it has a specific, defined, identified purpose. Its purpose is to provide a specific service from a trained, credentialed person with professional status. Psychotherapy is a specialty in helping people change their thoughts, feelings and/or behavior. In return for that help, the professional person is compensated for their time, skill and knowledge. Because it is a professional relationship, the therapy relationship has certain restrictions, limits and boundaries. Those restrictions, limits and boundaries create a focus for the therapy service and provide the client a high degree of safety from financial and personal exploitation. For a more detailed discussion about these factors, you can always talk to your therapist. Spending some time talking with your therapist about the boundaries of your therapy is generally a positive experience that can assist the change process.

In addition to the restrictions, limits and boundaries of the therapeutic relationship, there are several other important elements. These elements include the "fit" between you and your therapist, interventions, the clinical contract, and finally, the therapeutic alliance.

C. Fit

The fit refers to how well, in a natural way, the client and therapist seem to "understand" and "work" together. A good fit happens when two people verbally communicate in a way that just seems to make it easy to understand each other. Connecting is easy. The therapist and patient just seem to "hit it off" and there is an easy flow to the conversation. Something just seems to "click." No one is quite sure **why** it happens, but it does. There is now imaging that shows **what** lights up in our brain when it is happening.

In everyday life, a **"good fit"** seems to be mostly random. In some cases, people will "work" on a relationship in an effort to improve the fit. In the psychotherapy setting, it is reasonable to expect your therapist will have, as part of their professional repertoire, relationship-building skills. Having those skills, coupled with training and experience, to some extent, takes some of the randomness out of the development of a therapeutic relationship. The therapeutic relationship between you and your therapist is crucial to your therapy process. The therapeutic relationship provides the basis and focus for whatever problems or issues you want to address. Having a good working relationship with your psychotherapist is going to be very important to having successful therapy. With the establishment of the relationship, the identification of the problems/issues, and a sense the fit and feel, between you and the therapist is good, the therapy and/or counseling process is now ready to transition to the on-going phase.

•

D. Contract/Alliance Contract

The therapeutic alliance and contract refers to the "working" partnership between you and your therapist. Clients enter therapy seeking help to solve a psychological or relational problem they are experiencing. Clients assume that therapists have specific skills that will help them discover better, more effective ways of coping. But the help and change you are seeking is the result of **your effort combined with the therapist's skills.** The change you are seeking is a result of a team effort with you and your therapist working together. This effort is the basis of the **alliance** and is one of the keys to your success in therapy. The **alliance** refers to the general quality and strength of your working relationship with the therapist. The alliance also refers to the "feeling" between you and the therapist. Do you feel safe, comfortable, relaxed, understood, supported, etc.? Does it feel like the goals you had for seeking therapy are being met? While the alliance is a more general description of the working therapy relationship, **contracting** tends to focus on more specific activities.

Contracting refers to specific action agreements developed and agreed upon by you and your therapist. These agreements have at least three parts. The first part of the contracting process in the development of interventions. An intervention can be used or tried in or outside of the therapy room. After the development of an intervention the client then tries using the intervention. The final part of the contracting process is the evaluation of the effectivenss of the intervention. The evaluation of the effectiveness of the intervention is usually conducted in the therapy room with the therapist.

E. Intervention

The word *intervention* is a common word used during the psychotherapy process. Simply, interventions are planned courses of action. These interventions can be planned individually by you or your therapist. Interventions can also be jointly planned. Interventions are directed toward your external life or your internal life. Your external life includes work, family, friends, etc. Often at the end of a session a specific intervention might be identified for action. For example, it might be decided that you should become more assertive in a particular, personal relationship. In our internal world, interventions may be directed at the way we think or feel about some aspect of ourselves, someone else or a situation. While there is certainly spontaneity in the therapy room, sometimes the therapist will plan for a particular moment in a session to ask a specific question. The question may be intended for us to think about a situation in a different way. Interventions can be either verbal or behavioral.

F. Ending Psychotherapy

The ending of your therapy treatment, sometimes referred to as termination, will ideally be a joint process between you and your therapist. The ending phase usually takes two sessions, but sometimes more. The ending of the therapy can be initiated by either you or the therapist and usually signals that the goals you had when you started therapy have been met. In some cases, and usually this is rare, there may come a point where there is "no movement" in the therapy. This nonmovement is sometimes referred to as an impasse. When an impasse is encountered, there are usually several attempts to move beyond it. But if there is no success in breaking the impasse, then the therapy very well might end. Almost always before the therapy ends, at the very least, some, if not all, of the clients' goals are met.

Either you or your therapist will initiate the process of ending the psychotherapy. One of you will bring up ending the therapy, and that will spark a discussion. This discussion will include a review of what has been accomplished, and perhaps what has not been. **Usually discussed is what changed and how it changed.** Additionally, the therapist will ask for feedback on how you think he or she was helpful or perhaps not. It is important to give that feedback and for you to have your voice heard.

One final note. Most often today, the "ending" of therapy is seen as a phase. Indeed, the therapy may end and you may never seek therapy again. But what is at least equally likely to happen is that in the future, you will again enter therapy and continue to learn new ways of relating and coping. Thus, the therapist may say, "if something comes up, you are welcome to come back."

IV. Change: Self-Awareness, Self-Regulation, Assertiveness, Coping Skills and Emotional Intelligence

By far, the most frequent reason why a person "goes into therapy" is because they want to change some aspect of their life. Many people say they are seeking relief from psychological distress, whether it is intrapsychic (an internalized feeling like depression or anxiety), an interpersonal or relationship issue or a combination of intrapsychic and interpersonal. They may want to improve a relationship, change the way they behave in a certain situation or manage their emotions in a more effective manner. Because people are seeking some type of change in their life, often the first question a therapist will ask is "Why are you here?" Your answer will begin to reveal at least some of the reasons you have sought the assistance of a therapist. This beginning to your therapy will help you and the therapist create the "therapeutic contract." This contract begins to define the direction for your therapy and how the two of you will work together. Bringing about change in your life will usually impact your personal self-awareness, self-regulation, assertiveness and coping skills. As you review these aspects of change, you will quickly see the relationship between them all.

A. Self-Awareness

When we are in a situation of stress or distress, understanding why and how we react to it requires an understanding of ourselves. When we are trying to understand ourselves we look inside and attempt to identify why we might have said something, or behaved in a particular way. Or maybe we are trying to understand our reaction to an event or person. Increasing our understanding of ourselves will help us to identify what we do well and not so well. This knowledge is empowering and sheds light on our thoughts, feelings and behavior. **The elements of self-awareness include what we do (behaviors), our personal values and social goals (thoughts) and the internal reactions and results we experience (feelings).** Additionally, understanding ourselves helps us to understand others and greatly increases our ability to be empathetic and understand how other people feel. A review of the various aspects of your life is usually conducted. As we examine ourselves we will address issues about self-appraisal, how we function with others and within our roles in the community, at school or work.

B. Self-Regulation

Self-regulation is the ability to identify healthy personal goals and needs and direct ourselves to reach them. We are able to stay focused on meeting needs and goals and to **self-regulate** ourselves in whatever situation or environment we are in. To be successful at self-regulation, we must be ***aware*** of our strenghts and weaknesses. Moreover, we must be clear about our goals and to honestly monitor and evalute how successful we are at meeting them. Often we will have to develop new skills or improve old skills in order to better self-regulate ourselves. These skills include the ability to stay focused, and to evaluate how well we are doing in meeting our goals. Self-regulation also includes the ability to develop and secure resources which are needed. Moreover, self-regulation is critical during high-stress times so that we select an appropriate response to address different situations. When a person can self-regulate, they realize they have coping options, and they use them.

C. Assertiveness

In creating change in ourselves or our lives, the ability to express and communicate our needs is essential to good psychological health and functioning. There are three factors that are required if a person is to be assertive. One, is having the insight and skill to identify a personal need; two, is the skill to communicate that need; and three, is having the personal confidence and inner strength to actually convey a need to a person or a group. Assertiveness is not done with a disregard for other people's needs, and the communication of needs is done in a manner that balances the personal pursuit of getting a need met with respect for others. People can become assertive without being aggressive.

D. Coping Skills

One of the most important goals of your therapy will be to learn new coping skills. But what are coping skills? Simply put, coping skills are problem-solving skills we use to cope with stress and the problems of daily life. Generally, the stress you have identified to work on in your therapy will be found in social, work and family relationships, environmental situations and/or areas of significant life change. An example of an **environmental situation** might be a layoff at work, a robbery or a natural catastrophe, like Hurricane Katrina. **Significant life changes,** often referred to as life transitions, include the change of a job, divorce, retirement, etc. Our ability to understand, live with, manage and/or eliminate these stresses will go a long way in making for an effective therapy experience and an improved quality of life. Improving coping skills includes understanding the problem and finding a better solution to addressing it.

E. Emotional Intelligence

DEVELOPING EMOTIONAL INTELLIGENCE

In the past, it was enough to have a cognitive storehouse of information to get along in the world. Today, one needs what has been termed **emotional intelligence**. It has been defined as self-awareness, understanding or simply the demonstration of appropriate sensitivity for another person. Within the task of the psychotherapeutic relationship, frequently therapist and patient are looking at various ways to make interpersonal relationships work. Different interpersonal relationships take place both in one's personal life as well as their professional life. Obviously, being successful in both of those domains can lead a person to a higher level of peace, happiness and success.

A person who has acquired emotional intelligence is very astute to the cues, both verbal and nonverbal, of other people. Thus, they are skilled at sending and receiving messages from others with an ample amount of demonstrated concern and empathy. A therapist demonstrates emotional intelligence if he or she is able to join with the patient and the patient feels understood and good about the "doctor-patient" relationship. In any interaction where good emotional intelligence is operating, the two parties feel that there is a flow and symmetry in the emotional connection between the two people. In a psychotherapeutic relationship, which is indeed satisfying to both the patient as well as the therapist, there are several qualities which manifest themselves. These include:

- **A self-awareness where the two individuals "tune in" with their personal rhythms.**
- **Both parties demonstrate appropriate self-control. The clinician can deal with all of the emotions that are being presented by the patient. Conversely, the patient is learning ways to deal with the emotions that they experience day to day, thus being able to interact in a more positive fashion outside of therapy.**
- **The awareness of cues from others sometimes becomes a goal of therapy. Individuals who come into therapy might not be able to adequately read the cues of people in their lives which could result in conflict. In treatment, one can learn more effective ways of understanding others, reading interpersonal cues from others and learning appropriate ways to respond. Emotional intelligence can be a tool to learn for the patient to utilize across many situations; thus, one can learn how to generalize the utilization of their sensitivity and awareness with loved ones, colleagues, as well as business relationships.**

While many individuals have utilized the term "emotional intelligence," it came to national prominence with the 1995 book written by Dr. Daniel Goleman, titled *Emotional Intelligence.* According to Goleman (1995), the emotional information processing that was presented by earlier psychologist actually made what he now calls **emotional intelligence** popular. Currently, a four-branch model of emotional intelligence was put together by Mayer and Salovey (1997).

What one might seek in therapy can be seen in these four models that include:

1. Managing Emotions

People sometimes will present themselves to the psychotherapist stating that, "I saw red and lost control of myself." Therapy is a place where one can understand that emotional regulation is possible through acquiring information, identifying one's personal triggers and understanding there are more ways of responding to a dilemma than one. Thus, the patient can have a better grasp of ways where they can effectively control themselves and respond to others without generating one crisis into another.

2. Understanding Emotions

When we accurately read another person's emotions, we are then getting the message which is attempted to be conveyed to us in a greater than cognitive fashion. For example, understanding all nuances of anger, frustration, disappointment or happiness is an important skill to acquire through the psychotherapeutic relationship.

3. Facilitating Thought

In understanding emotions, we can then do a better job to guide our understanding of the other person and put together a better response to any type of interaction. You can think of this as the input aspect for making a decision about how to relate to another person, which can be considered the output aspect.

4. Perceiving Emotions

Dr. Goleman thought of it as the most basic area of both receiving and expressing emotion. The verbal and nonverbal bits of information that are in any interaction helps you better understand through both the nonverbal and verbal starting point of understanding emotions.

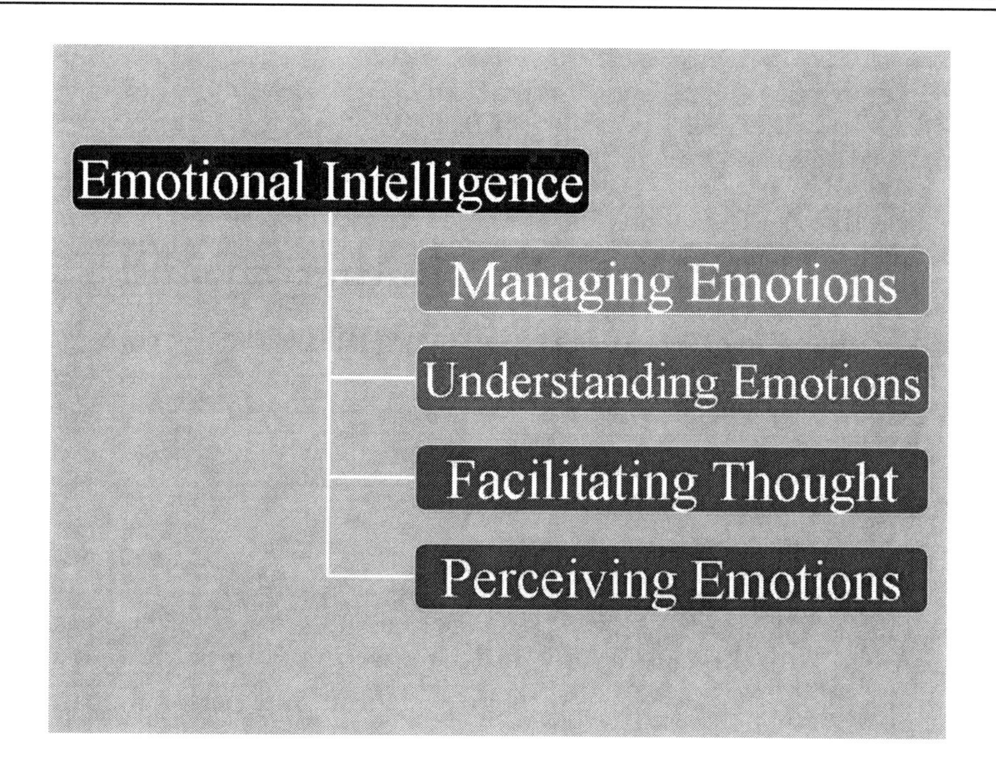

THE FOUR-BRANCH MODEL OF EMOTIONAL INTELLIGENCE
(after Goleman, 1995)

Once an individual has learned to understand the different aspects, or branches, of emotional intelligence, then they may do a better job in acquiring the skills to control and enhance their own emotional intelligence. Thus, this is all a part of emotionally helping to bring your life into better balance.

V. Using Your Psychotherapy and Counseling Companion

Our goal in creating **"Your Psychotherapy and Counseling Companion"** is to provide you with an easy to use, concrete tool that can help you meet your personal goals more quickly and more effectively. We envision "Your Companion" as a bridge that helps you use what you learned in your therapy session into your everyday life. Your Companion is a written resource and reference, an observer, of your therapy experience. Bring Your Companion to each of your therapy sessions and use the strategies, information and increased self-awareness to live a more satisfying life.

In the body of "The Companion" the reader will find three types of session forms. On all three types of forms you have the opportunity to record the session date, name of therapist and people present. The specifics of what to include in each type of session are as follows:

A. First in Session

You will find only one copy of this form.

1. Write down the reasons, problems and issues that caused you to contact a therapist and begin psychotherapy or counseling.

2. Write down the goals you have for your therapy. What results would you like to achieve.

3. Rate how comfortable you feel with the therapist. Do you seem to "connect" with them and they with you?

B. Weekly or On-Going Therapy Sessions

Included are 50 copies of this form. However, you are welcome to make as many copies of this form as necessary.

1. Review and document in The Comapnion any changes, significant events, thoughts, feelings, issues or problems you experienced since your last session.

2. Assess how you feel, or think, the therapy is progressing. Is the therapy focusing on what you want to change or accomplish?

3. At the end of the session you and your therapist should take a few minutes to review and write down the key points and recommendations from the session. Review what activities and/or interventions are to be implemented or what thoughts might be reflected upon. Remember, sometimes patients/clients may simply be asked to consider a thought or belief they may have.

C. Therapy /Counseling Ending Phase

There is only one copy of this form.

1. List your problem(s) or issues and rate to what extent your goal(s) was met.

2. Write out what you thought was most helpful about your therapy.

3. Write out suggestions of what could have helped you improve therapy.

4. Rate the therapy experience.

D. Out of Session

1. You should, if possible, review the session notes from **"The Companion"** as often as possible. Some of our clients have reviewed their notes every morning before they start their day. Others referred to their notes during the day whenever they have an opportunity. Others still use the book when a specific issue or problem arises. We believe your life and style will determine how you use the book. But like any tool, it is only useful when used and practiced!

2. Write down any thoughts, revelations or experiences that might be relevant to your therapy. Jot downs all insights or questions you might have.

As previously noted, **"Your Psychotherapy and Counseling Companion"** is intended to help you carry over experiences and information from your counseling sessions into your daily life. Further, **"The Companion"** is designed to be adaptable to your individual needs and style. To that end we encourage you and your therapist to use **"The Companion"** in a flexible and personal way that meets your special and unique therapy needs. Be a partner in your therapy and inform the therapist how you think your therapy is progressing. Communicate to them what seems to be working for you and what might not, be working. Most therapists will welcome and respect your feedback. Remember, with effort and the right professional help, you can achieve the goals you set for yourself and change your life.

E. Appendix Section

Included with **"The Companion"** is an index section that provides general information pertaining to medication, examples of "homework assignments" and a listing of resources for common issues or problems. If you are taking any medication, always check with your doctor or therapist with questions regarding the medication. In keeping with the overriding purpose of the book, space has been provided for your therapist to individualize information for you. **"The Companion"** provides a deliberate balance between offering direction, continuity and support, without intruding in the natural therapy process between you and your therapist.

"Your Psychotherapy Companion" is not a curriculum manual, nor does it provide specific clinical information, strategies or theory. Rather, it is your personal therapy assistant helping you retain vital information discussed in a therapy or counseling session. It is our hope **"The Companion"** will assist you on a daily basis, and help you more quickly and efficiently reach your therapy goals. And **"The Companion"** can also serve as a personal reference book after your psychotherapy and/or counseling has ended. A true journal of a unique experience.

And finally, always remember, it is critically important you feel comfortable with your therapist or counselor. It is imperative you feel safe and respected. Be sure to offer your thoughts and feelings about the direction and progress of your therapy to your therapist.

VI. Session Forms

First Session

Weekly or Ongoing Therapy Sessions

Therapy/Counseling Ending Phase

SESSION NOTES or THOUGHTS

First Session

SESSION DATE: ____________________NAME OF THERAPIST: ______________________
PEOPLE PRESENT IN SESSION: ____

ISSUE(S), PROBLEM(S) OR GOAL(S) THAT CAUSED YOU TO SEEK PSYCHOTHERAPY OR COUNSELING (These items are essential to establishing your contract with your therapist):

1. ____
____

2. ____
____

3. ____
____

REGARDING YOUR ISSUES OR PROBLEMS, WHAT CHANGE WOULD YOU LIKE?
____
____
____

RATE YOUR COMFORT LEVEL WITH THE THERAPIST:

VERY COMFORTABLE VERY UNCOMFORTABLE
10 9 8 7 6 5 4 3 2 1

WHAT COULD THE THERAPIST DO OR SAY TO BE MORE HELPFUL?
____
____

SESSION NOTES or THOUGHTS

Weekly or Ongoing Therapy Sessions

SESSION DATE: ____________________PEOPLE PRESENT: ______________________

WRITE DOWN ANY CHANGE, EVENT, ISSUE EXPERIENCE SINCE YOUR LAST SESSION: (Complete this prior to today's session)

____

____

____

WRITE A SENTENCE ABOUT WHAT YOU REMEMBER FROM THE LAST SESSION: (Complete this prior to today's session)

____

____

____

KEY POINTS OR ISSUES COVERED TODAY:

____

____

____

HOMEWORK OR THINGS TO THINK ABOUT BETWEEN NOW AND MY NEXT SESSION:

____

____

____

HELPFULNESS OF SESSION IN HELPING TO RESOLVE ISSUES, PROBLEMS or MEET GOALS

(make a check on this scale):

Extremely Helpful—--------l-------------l------------l----------Not Helpful at all

10 5 1

SESSION NOTES or THOUGHTS

Weekly or Ongoing Therapy Sessions

SESSION DATE: ____________________PEOPLE PRESENT: ______________________

WRITE DOWN ANY CHANGE, EVENT, ISSUE EXPERIENCE SINCE YOUR LAST SESSION: (Complete this prior to today's session)

____

____

____

WRITE A SENTENCE ABOUT WHAT YOU REMEMBER FROM THE LAST SESSION: (Complete this prior to today's session)

____

____

____

KEY POINTS OR ISSUES COVERED TODAY:

____

____

____

HOMEWORK OR THINGS TO THINK ABOUT BETWEEN NOW AND MY NEXT SESSION:

____

____

____

HELPFULNESS OF SESSION IN HELPING TO RESOLVE ISSUES, PROBLEMS or MEET GOALS

(make a check on this scale):

Extremely Helpful—--------l-------------l------------l----------Not Helpful at all

10 5 1

SESSION NOTES or THOUGHTS

Weekly or Ongoing Therapy Sessions

SESSION DATE: ____________________PEOPLE PRESENT: ______________________

WRITE DOWN ANY CHANGE, EVENT, ISSUE EXPERIENCE SINCE YOUR LAST SESSION: (Complete this prior to today's session)

___

___

___

WRITE A SENTENCE ABOUT WHAT YOU REMEMBER FROM THE LAST SESSION: (Complete this prior to today's session)

___

___

___

KEY POINTS OR ISSUES COVERED TODAY:

___

___

___

HOMEWORK OR THINGS TO THINK ABOUT BETWEEN NOW AND MY NEXT SESSION:

___

___

___

HELPFULNESS OF SESSION IN HELPING TO RESOLVE ISSUES, PROBLEMS or MEET GOALS

(make a check on this scale):

Extremely Helpful—--------|-------------|------------|----------Not Helpful at all

10 5 1

SESSION NOTES or THOUGHTS

Weekly or Ongoing Therapy Sessions

SESSION DATE: ____________________PEOPLE PRESENT: ______________________

WRITE DOWN ANY CHANGE, EVENT, ISSUE EXPERIENCE SINCE YOUR LAST SESSION: (Complete this prior to today's session)

____

____

____

WRITE A SENTENCE ABOUT WHAT YOU REMEMBER FROM THE LAST SESSION: (Complete this prior to today's session)

____

____

____

KEY POINTS OR ISSUES COVERED TODAY:

____

____

____

HOMEWORK OR THINGS TO THINK ABOUT BETWEEN NOW AND MY NEXT SESSION:

____

____

____

HELPFULNESS OF SESSION IN HELPING TO RESOLVE ISSUES, PROBLEMS or MEET GOALS

(make a check on this scale):

Extremely Helpful—--------|-------------|------------|----------Not Helpful at all

10 5 1

SESSION NOTES or THOUGHTS

Weekly or Ongoing Therapy Sessions

SESSION DATE: ____________________ PEOPLE PRESENT: ______________________

WRITE DOWN ANY CHANGE, EVENT, ISSUE EXPERIENCE SINCE YOUR LAST SESSION: (Complete this prior to today's session)

____

____

____

WRITE A SENTENCE ABOUT WHAT YOU REMEMBER FROM THE LAST SESSION: (Complete this prior to today's session)

____

____

____

KEY POINTS OR ISSUES COVERED TODAY:

____

____

____

HOMEWORK OR THINGS TO THINK ABOUT BETWEEN NOW AND MY NEXT SESSION:

____

____

____

HELPFULNESS OF SESSION IN HELPING TO RESOLVE ISSUES, PROBLEMS or MEET GOALS

(make a check on this scale):

Extremely Helpful—--------|-------------|------------|----------Not Helpful at all

10 5 1

SESSION NOTES or THOUGHTS

Weekly or Ongoing Therapy Sessions

SESSION DATE: ____________________PEOPLE PRESENT: ________________________

WRITE DOWN ANY CHANGE, EVENT, ISSUE EXPERIENCE SINCE YOUR LAST SESSION: (Complete this prior to today's session)

____

____

____

WRITE A SENTENCE ABOUT WHAT YOU REMEMBER FROM THE LAST SESSION: (Complete this prior to today's session)

____

____

____

KEY POINTS OR ISSUES COVERED TODAY:

____

____

____

HOMEWORK OR THINGS TO THINK ABOUT BETWEEN NOW AND MY NEXT SESSION:

____

____

____

HELPFULNESS OF SESSION IN HELPING TO RESOLVE ISSUES, PROBLEMS or MEET GOALS

(make a check on this scale):

Extremely Helpful—--------l-------------l------------l----------Not Helpful at all

10 5 1

SESSION NOTES or THOUGHTS

Weekly or Ongoing Therapy Sessions

SESSION DATE: ____________________PEOPLE PRESENT: ______________________

WRITE DOWN ANY CHANGE, EVENT, ISSUE EXPERIENCE SINCE YOUR LAST SESSION: (Complete this prior to today's session)

____

____

____

WRITE A SENTENCE ABOUT WHAT YOU REMEMBER FROM THE LAST SESSION: (Complete this prior to today's session)

____

____

____

KEY POINTS OR ISSUES COVERED TODAY:

____

____

____

HOMEWORK OR THINGS TO THINK ABOUT BETWEEN NOW AND MY NEXT SESSION:

____

____

____

HELPFULNESS OF SESSION IN HELPING TO RESOLVE ISSUES, PROBLEMS or MEET GOALS

(make a check on this scale):

Extremely Helpful———-------|-------------|------------|----------Not Helpful at all

10 5 1

SESSION NOTES or THOUGHTS

Weekly or Ongoing Therapy Sessions

SESSION DATE: ____________________PEOPLE PRESENT: ________________________

WRITE DOWN ANY CHANGE, EVENT, ISSUE EXPERIENCE SINCE YOUR LAST SESSION: (Complete this prior to today's session)

____

____

____

WRITE A SENTENCE ABOUT WHAT YOU REMEMBER FROM THE LAST SESSION: (Complete this prior to today's session)

____

____

____

KEY POINTS OR ISSUES COVERED TODAY:

____

____

____

HOMEWORK OR THINGS TO THINK ABOUT BETWEEN NOW AND MY NEXT SESSION:

____

____

____

HELPFULNESS OF SESSION IN HELPING TO RESOLVE ISSUES, PROBLEMS or MEET GOALS

(make a check on this scale):

Extremely Helpful——--------l-------------l------------l----------Not Helpful at all

10 5 1

SESSION NOTES or THOUGHTS

Weekly or Ongoing Therapy Sessions

SESSION DATE: ____________________ PEOPLE PRESENT: ______________________

WRITE DOWN ANY CHANGE, EVENT, ISSUE EXPERIENCE SINCE YOUR LAST SESSION: (Complete this prior to today's session)

____

____

____

WRITE A SENTENCE ABOUT WHAT YOU REMEMBER FROM THE LAST SESSION: (Complete this prior to today's session)

____

____

____

KEY POINTS OR ISSUES COVERED TODAY:

____

____

____

HOMEWORK OR THINGS TO THINK ABOUT BETWEEN NOW AND MY NEXT SESSION:

____

____

____

HELPFULNESS OF SESSION IN HELPING TO RESOLVE ISSUES, PROBLEMS or MEET GOALS

(make a check on this scale):

Extremely Helpful———--------|------------|-----------|----------Not Helpful at all

10 5 1

SESSION NOTES or THOUGHTS

Weekly or Ongoing Therapy Sessions

SESSION DATE: ____________________PEOPLE PRESENT: ______________________

WRITE DOWN ANY CHANGE, EVENT, ISSUE EXPERIENCE SINCE YOUR LAST SESSION: (Complete this prior to today's session)

____

____

____

WRITE A SENTENCE ABOUT WHAT YOU REMEMBER FROM THE LAST SESSION: (Complete this prior to today's session)

____

____

____

KEY POINTS OR ISSUES COVERED TODAY:

____

____

____

HOMEWORK OR THINGS TO THINK ABOUT BETWEEN NOW AND MY NEXT SESSION:

____

____

____

HELPFULNESS OF SESSION IN HELPING TO RESOLVE ISSUES, PROBLEMS or MEET GOALS

(make a check on this scale):

Extremely Helpful—--------|------------|-----------|----------Not Helpful at all

10 5 1

SESSION NOTES or THOUGHTS

Weekly or Ongoing Therapy Sessions

SESSION DATE: ____________________ PEOPLE PRESENT: ____________________

WRITE DOWN ANY CHANGE, EVENT, ISSUE EXPERIENCE SINCE YOUR LAST SESSION: (Complete this prior to today's session)

____

____

____

WRITE A SENTENCE ABOUT WHAT YOU REMEMBER FROM THE LAST SESSION: (Complete this prior to today's session)

____

____

____

KEY POINTS OR ISSUES COVERED TODAY:

____

____

____

HOMEWORK OR THINGS TO THINK ABOUT BETWEEN NOW AND MY NEXT SESSION:

____

____

____

HELPFULNESS OF SESSION IN HELPING TO RESOLVE ISSUES, PROBLEMS or MEET GOALS

(make a check on this scale):

Extremely Helpful—--------l-------------l------------l----------Not Helpful at all

10 5 1

<u>SESSION NOTES or THOUGHTS</u>

Weekly or Ongoing Therapy Sessions

SESSION DATE: ____________________PEOPLE PRESENT: ________________________

WRITE DOWN ANY CHANGE, EVENT, ISSUE EXPERIENCE SINCE YOUR LAST SESSION: (Complete this prior to today's session)

____

____

____

WRITE A SENTENCE ABOUT WHAT YOU REMEMBER FROM THE LAST SESSION: (Complete this prior to today's session)

____

____

____

KEY POINTS OR ISSUES COVERED TODAY:

____

____

____

HOMEWORK OR THINGS TO THINK ABOUT BETWEEN NOW AND MY NEXT SESSION:

____

____

____

HELPFULNESS OF SESSION IN HELPING TO RESOLVE ISSUES, PROBLEMS or MEET GOALS

(make a check on this scale):

Extremely Helpful————l------------l-----------l----------Not Helpful at all

10 5 1

SESSION NOTES or THOUGHTS

Weekly or Ongoing Therapy Sessions

SESSION DATE: ____________________PEOPLE PRESENT: ______________________

WRITE DOWN ANY CHANGE, EVENT, ISSUE EXPERIENCE SINCE YOUR LAST SESSION: (Complete this prior to today's session)

____

____

____

WRITE A SENTENCE ABOUT WHAT YOU REMEMBER FROM THE LAST SESSION: (Complete this prior to today's session)

____

____

____

KEY POINTS OR ISSUES COVERED TODAY:

____

____

____

HOMEWORK OR THINGS TO THINK ABOUT BETWEEN NOW AND MY NEXT SESSION:

____

____

____

HELPFULNESS OF SESSION IN HELPING TO RESOLVE ISSUES, PROBLEMS or MEET GOALS

(make a check on this scale):

Extremely Helpful————-l-------------l------------l----------Not Helpful at all

10 5 1

SESSION NOTES or THOUGHTS

Weekly or Ongoing Therapy Sessions

SESSION DATE: ____________________PEOPLE PRESENT: ________________________

WRITE DOWN ANY CHANGE, EVENT, ISSUE EXPERIENCE SINCE YOUR LAST SESSION: (Complete this prior to today's session)

____

____

____

WRITE A SENTENCE ABOUT WHAT YOU REMEMBER FROM THE LAST SESSION: (Complete this prior to today's session)

____

____

____

KEY POINTS OR ISSUES COVERED TODAY:

____

____

____

HOMEWORK OR THINGS TO THINK ABOUT BETWEEN NOW AND MY NEXT SESSION:

____

____

____

HELPFULNESS OF SESSION IN HELPING TO RESOLVE ISSUES, PROBLEMS or MEET GOALS

(make a check on this scale):

Extremely Helpful—--------|-------------|------------|----------Not Helpful at all

10 5 1

SESSION NOTES or THOUGHTS

Weekly or Ongoing Therapy Sessions

SESSION DATE: ____________________PEOPLE PRESENT: ________________________

WRITE DOWN ANY CHANGE, EVENT, ISSUE EXPERIENCE SINCE YOUR LAST SESSION: (Complete this prior to today's session)

____

____

____

WRITE A SENTENCE ABOUT WHAT YOU REMEMBER FROM THE LAST SESSION: (Complete this prior to today's session)

____

____

____

KEY POINTS OR ISSUES COVERED TODAY:

____

____

____

HOMEWORK OR THINGS TO THINK ABOUT BETWEEN NOW AND MY NEXT SESSION:

____

____

____

HELPFULNESS OF SESSION IN HELPING TO RESOLVE ISSUES, PROBLEMS or MEET GOALS

(make a check on this scale):

Extremely Helpful—--------l-------------l------------l----------Not Helpful at all

10 5 1

SESSION NOTES or THOUGHTS

Weekly or Ongoing Therapy Sessions

SESSION DATE: ____________________PEOPLE PRESENT: ______________________

WRITE DOWN ANY CHANGE, EVENT, ISSUE EXPERIENCE SINCE YOUR LAST SESSION: (Complete this prior to today's session)

____

____

____

WRITE A SENTENCE ABOUT WHAT YOU REMEMBER FROM THE LAST SESSION: (Complete this prior to today's session)

____

____

____

KEY POINTS OR ISSUES COVERED TODAY:

____

____

____

HOMEWORK OR THINGS TO THINK ABOUT BETWEEN NOW AND MY NEXT SESSION:

____

____

____

HELPFULNESS OF SESSION IN HELPING TO RESOLVE ISSUES, PROBLEMS or MEET GOALS

(make a check on this scale):

Extremely Helpful—--------|------------|-----------|---------Not Helpful at all

10 5 1

SESSION NOTES or THOUGHTS

Weekly or Ongoing Therapy Sessions

SESSION DATE: ____________________PEOPLE PRESENT: ________________________

WRITE DOWN ANY CHANGE, EVENT, ISSUE EXPERIENCE SINCE YOUR LAST SESSION: (Complete this prior to today's session)

____

____

____

WRITE A SENTENCE ABOUT WHAT YOU REMEMBER FROM THE LAST SESSION: (Complete this prior to today's session)

____

____

____

KEY POINTS OR ISSUES COVERED TODAY:

____

____

____

HOMEWORK OR THINGS TO THINK ABOUT BETWEEN NOW AND MY NEXT SESSION:

____

____

____

HELPFULNESS OF SESSION IN HELPING TO RESOLVE ISSUES, PROBLEMS or MEET GOALS

(make a check on this scale):

Extremely Helpful—---------l-------------l------------l----------Not Helpful at all

10 5 1

SESSION NOTES or THOUGHTS

Weekly or Ongoing Therapy Sessions

SESSION DATE: ____________________PEOPLE PRESENT: ________________________

WRITE DOWN ANY CHANGE, EVENT, ISSUE EXPERIENCE SINCE YOUR LAST SESSION: (Complete this prior to today's session)

____

____

____

WRITE A SENTENCE ABOUT WHAT YOU REMEMBER FROM THE LAST SESSION: (Complete this prior to today's session)

____

____

____

KEY POINTS OR ISSUES COVERED TODAY:

____

____

____

HOMEWORK OR THINGS TO THINK ABOUT BETWEEN NOW AND MY NEXT SESSION:

____

____

____

HELPFULNESS OF SESSION IN HELPING TO RESOLVE ISSUES, PROBLEMS or MEET GOALS

(make a check on this scale):

Extremely Helpful—--------|-------------|------------|----------Not Helpful at all

10 5 1

SESSION NOTES or THOUGHTS

Weekly or Ongoing Therapy Sessions

SESSION DATE: ____________________PEOPLE PRESENT: ______________________

WRITE DOWN ANY CHANGE, EVENT, ISSUE EXPERIENCE SINCE YOUR LAST SESSION: (Complete this prior to today's session)

___

___

___

WRITE A SENTENCE ABOUT WHAT YOU REMEMBER FROM THE LAST SESSION: (Complete this prior to today's session)

___

___

___

KEY POINTS OR ISSUES COVERED TODAY:

___

___

___

HOMEWORK OR THINGS TO THINK ABOUT BETWEEN NOW AND MY NEXT SESSION:

___

___

___

HELPFULNESS OF SESSION IN HELPING TO RESOLVE ISSUES, PROBLEMS or MEET GOALS

(make a check on this scale):

Extremely Helpful—--------l-------------l------------l----------Not Helpful at all

10 5 1

SESSION NOTES or THOUGHTS

Weekly or Ongoing Therapy Sessions

SESSION DATE: ____________________PEOPLE PRESENT: ________________________

WRITE DOWN ANY CHANGE, EVENT, ISSUE EXPERIENCE SINCE YOUR LAST SESSION: (Complete this prior to today's session)

____
____
____

WRITE A SENTENCE ABOUT WHAT YOU REMEMBER FROM THE LAST SESSION: (Complete this prior to today's session)

____
____
____

KEY POINTS OR ISSUES COVERED TODAY:

____
____
____

HOMEWORK OR THINGS TO THINK ABOUT BETWEEN NOW AND MY NEXT SESSION:

____
____
____

HELPFULNESS OF SESSION IN HELPING TO RESOLVE ISSUES, PROBLEMS or MEET GOALS

(make a check on this scale):

Extremely Helpful——--------|------------|-----------|----------Not Helpful at all

10 5 1

SESSION NOTES or THOUGHTS

Weekly or Ongoing Therapy Sessions

SESSION DATE: ____________________PEOPLE PRESENT: ____________________

WRITE DOWN ANY CHANGE, EVENT, ISSUE EXPERIENCE SINCE YOUR LAST SESSION: (Complete this prior to today's session)

____

____

____

WRITE A SENTENCE ABOUT WHAT YOU REMEMBER FROM THE LAST SESSION: (Complete this prior to today's session)

____

____

____

KEY POINTS OR ISSUES COVERED TODAY:

____

____

____

HOMEWORK OR THINGS TO THINK ABOUT BETWEEN NOW AND MY NEXT SESSION:

____

____

____

HELPFULNESS OF SESSION IN HELPING TO RESOLVE ISSUES, PROBLEMS or MEET GOALS

(make a check on this scale):

Extremely Helpful—--------|-------------|------------|----------Not Helpful at all

10 5 1

SESSION NOTES or THOUGHTS

Weekly or Ongoing Therapy Sessions

SESSION DATE: ____________________ PEOPLE PRESENT: ______________________

WRITE DOWN ANY CHANGE, EVENT, ISSUE EXPERIENCE SINCE YOUR LAST SESSION: (Complete this prior to today's session)

____

____

____

WRITE A SENTENCE ABOUT WHAT YOU REMEMBER FROM THE LAST SESSION: (Complete this prior to today's session)

____

____

____

KEY POINTS OR ISSUES COVERED TODAY:

____

____

____

HOMEWORK OR THINGS TO THINK ABOUT BETWEEN NOW AND MY NEXT SESSION:

____

____

____

HELPFULNESS OF SESSION IN HELPING TO RESOLVE ISSUES, PROBLEMS or MEET GOALS

(make a check on this scale):

Extremely Helpful—--------|------------|-----------|----------Not Helpful at all

10 5 1

SESSION NOTES or THOUGHTS

Weekly or Ongoing Therapy Sessions

SESSION DATE: ____________________PEOPLE PRESENT: ________________________

WRITE DOWN ANY CHANGE, EVENT, ISSUE EXPERIENCE SINCE YOUR LAST SESSION: (Complete this prior to today's session)

____

____

____

WRITE A SENTENCE ABOUT WHAT YOU REMEMBER FROM THE LAST SESSION: (Complete this prior to today's session)

____

____

____

KEY POINTS OR ISSUES COVERED TODAY:

____

____

____

HOMEWORK OR THINGS TO THINK ABOUT BETWEEN NOW AND MY NEXT SESSION:

____

____

____

HELPFULNESS OF SESSION IN HELPING TO RESOLVE ISSUES, PROBLEMS or MEET GOALS

(make a check on this scale):

Extremely Helpful———-------l------------l-----------l----------Not Helpful at all

10 5 1

SESSION NOTES or THOUGHTS

Weekly or Ongoing Therapy Sessions

SESSION DATE: ____________________PEOPLE PRESENT: ________________________

WRITE DOWN ANY CHANGE, EVENT, ISSUE EXPERIENCE SINCE YOUR LAST SESSION: (Complete this prior to today's session)

____

____

____

WRITE A SENTENCE ABOUT WHAT YOU REMEMBER FROM THE LAST SESSION: (Complete this prior to today's session)

____

____

____

KEY POINTS OR ISSUES COVERED TODAY:

____

____

____

HOMEWORK OR THINGS TO THINK ABOUT BETWEEN NOW AND MY NEXT SESSION:

____

____

____

HELPFULNESS OF SESSION IN HELPING TO RESOLVE ISSUES, PROBLEMS or MEET GOALS

(make a check on this scale):

Extremely Helpful—--------|-------------|------------|----------Not Helpful at all

10 5 1

SESSION NOTES or THOUGHTS

Weekly or Ongoing Therapy Sessions

SESSION DATE: ____________________PEOPLE PRESENT: ______________________

WRITE DOWN ANY CHANGE, EVENT, ISSUE EXPERIENCE SINCE YOUR LAST SESSION: (Complete this prior to today's session)

____

____

____

WRITE A SENTENCE ABOUT WHAT YOU REMEMBER FROM THE LAST SESSION: (Complete this prior to today's session)

____

____

____

KEY POINTS OR ISSUES COVERED TODAY:

____

____

____

HOMEWORK OR THINGS TO THINK ABOUT BETWEEN NOW AND MY NEXT SESSION:

____

____

____

HELPFULNESS OF SESSION IN HELPING TO RESOLVE ISSUES, PROBLEMS or MEET GOALS

(make a check on this scale):

Extremely Helpful—--------|-------------|------------|----------Not Helpful at all

10 5 1

SESSION NOTES or THOUGHTS

Weekly or Ongoing Therapy Sessions

SESSION DATE: ____________________PEOPLE PRESENT: ________________________

WRITE DOWN ANY CHANGE, EVENT, ISSUE EXPERIENCE SINCE YOUR LAST SESSION: (Complete this prior to today's session)

____

____

____

WRITE A SENTENCE ABOUT WHAT YOU REMEMBER FROM THE LAST SESSION: (Complete this prior to today's session)

____

____

____

KEY POINTS OR ISSUES COVERED TODAY:

____

____

____

HOMEWORK OR THINGS TO THINK ABOUT BETWEEN NOW AND MY NEXT SESSION:

____

____

____

HELPFULNESS OF SESSION IN HELPING TO RESOLVE ISSUES, PROBLEMS or MEET GOALS

(make a check on this scale):

Extremely Helpful—--------l-------------l------------l----------Not Helpful at all

10 5 1

SESSION NOTES or THOUGHTS

Weekly or Ongoing Therapy Sessions

SESSION DATE: ____________________PEOPLE PRESENT: ______________________

WRITE DOWN ANY CHANGE, EVENT, ISSUE EXPERIENCE SINCE YOUR LAST SESSION: (Complete this prior to today's session)

____

____

____

WRITE A SENTENCE ABOUT WHAT YOU REMEMBER FROM THE LAST SESSION: (Complete this prior to today's session)

____

____

____

KEY POINTS OR ISSUES COVERED TODAY:

____

____

____

HOMEWORK OR THINGS TO THINK ABOUT BETWEEN NOW AND MY NEXT SESSION:

____

____

____

HELPFULNESS OF SESSION IN HELPING TO RESOLVE ISSUES, PROBLEMS or MEET GOALS

(make a check on this scale):

Extremely Helpful——--------l-------------l------------l----------Not Helpful at all

10 5 1

SESSION NOTES or THOUGHTS

Weekly or Ongoing Therapy Sessions

SESSION DATE: ____________________PEOPLE PRESENT: ________________________

WRITE DOWN ANY CHANGE, EVENT, ISSUE EXPERIENCE SINCE YOUR LAST SESSION: (Complete this prior to today's session)

____

____

____

WRITE A SENTENCE ABOUT WHAT YOU REMEMBER FROM THE LAST SESSION: (Complete this prior to today's session)

____

____

____

KEY POINTS OR ISSUES COVERED TODAY:

____

____

____

HOMEWORK OR THINGS TO THINK ABOUT BETWEEN NOW AND MY NEXT SESSION:

____

____

____

HELPFULNESS OF SESSION IN HELPING TO RESOLVE ISSUES, PROBLEMS or MEET GOALS

(make a check on this scale):

Extremely Helpful—--------l-------------l------------l----------Not Helpful at all

10 5 1

SESSION NOTES or THOUGHTS

Weekly or Ongoing Therapy Sessions

SESSION DATE: ____________________PEOPLE PRESENT: ________________________

WRITE DOWN ANY CHANGE, EVENT, ISSUE EXPERIENCE SINCE YOUR LAST SESSION: (Complete this prior to today's session)

____

____

____

WRITE A SENTENCE ABOUT WHAT YOU REMEMBER FROM THE LAST SESSION: (Complete this prior to today's session)

____

____

____

KEY POINTS OR ISSUES COVERED TODAY:

____

____

____

HOMEWORK OR THINGS TO THINK ABOUT BETWEEN NOW AND MY NEXT SESSION:

____

____

____

HELPFULNESS OF SESSION IN HELPING TO RESOLVE ISSUES, PROBLEMS or MEET GOALS

(make a check on this scale):

Extremely Helpful—--------|-------------|------------|----------Not Helpful at all

10 5 1

SESSION NOTES or THOUGHTS

•

Weekly or Ongoing Therapy Sessions

SESSION DATE: ____________________ PEOPLE PRESENT: ________________________

WRITE DOWN ANY CHANGE, EVENT, ISSUE EXPERIENCE SINCE YOUR LAST SESSION: (Complete this prior to today's session)

____

____

____

WRITE A SENTENCE ABOUT WHAT YOU REMEMBER FROM THE LAST SESSION: (Complete this prior to today's session)

____

____

____

KEY POINTS OR ISSUES COVERED TODAY:

____

____

____

HOMEWORK OR THINGS TO THINK ABOUT BETWEEN NOW AND MY NEXT SESSION:

____

____

____

HELPFULNESS OF SESSION IN HELPING TO RESOLVE ISSUES, PROBLEMS or MEET GOALS

(make a check on this scale):

Extremely Helpful—--------|-------------|------------|----------Not Helpful at all

10 5 1

SESSION NOTES or THOUGHTS

Weekly or Ongoing Therapy Sessions

SESSION DATE: ____________________PEOPLE PRESENT: ________________________

WRITE DOWN ANY CHANGE, EVENT, ISSUE EXPERIENCE SINCE YOUR LAST SESSION: (Complete this prior to today's session)

____

____

____

WRITE A SENTENCE ABOUT WHAT YOU REMEMBER FROM THE LAST SESSION: (Complete this prior to today's session)

____

____

____

KEY POINTS OR ISSUES COVERED TODAY:

____

____

____

HOMEWORK OR THINGS TO THINK ABOUT BETWEEN NOW AND MY NEXT SESSION:

____

____

____

HELPFULNESS OF SESSION IN HELPING TO RESOLVE ISSUES, PROBLEMS or MEET GOALS

(make a check on this scale):

Extremely Helpful————-l------------l-----------l----------Not Helpful at all

10 5 1

SESSION NOTES or THOUGHTS

Weekly or Ongoing Therapy Sessions

SESSION DATE: ____________________ PEOPLE PRESENT: ________________________

WRITE DOWN ANY CHANGE, EVENT, ISSUE EXPERIENCE SINCE YOUR LAST SESSION: (Complete this prior to today's session)

____

____

____

WRITE A SENTENCE ABOUT WHAT YOU REMEMBER FROM THE LAST SESSION: (Complete this prior to today's session)

____

____

____

KEY POINTS OR ISSUES COVERED TODAY:

____

____

____

HOMEWORK OR THINGS TO THINK ABOUT BETWEEN NOW AND MY NEXT SESSION:

____

____

____

HELPFULNESS OF SESSION IN HELPING TO RESOLVE ISSUES, PROBLEMS or MEET GOALS

(make a check on this scale):

Extremely Helpful—--------l-------------l------------l----------Not Helpful at all

10 5 1

SESSION NOTES or THOUGHTS

Weekly or Ongoing Therapy Sessions

SESSION DATE: ____________________PEOPLE PRESENT: ________________________

WRITE DOWN ANY CHANGE, EVENT, ISSUE EXPERIENCE SINCE YOUR LAST SESSION: (Complete this prior to today's session)

____

____

____

WRITE A SENTENCE ABOUT WHAT YOU REMEMBER FROM THE LAST SESSION: (Complete this prior to today's session)

____

____

____

KEY POINTS OR ISSUES COVERED TODAY:

____

____

____

HOMEWORK OR THINGS TO THINK ABOUT BETWEEN NOW AND MY NEXT SESSION:

____

____

____

HELPFULNESS OF SESSION IN HELPING TO RESOLVE ISSUES, PROBLEMS or MEET GOALS

(make a check on this scale):

Extremely Helpful—--------l-------------l------------l----------Not Helpful at all

10 5 1

SESSION NOTES or THOUGHTS

Weekly or Ongoing Therapy Sessions

SESSION DATE: ____________________ PEOPLE PRESENT: ______________________

WRITE DOWN ANY CHANGE, EVENT, ISSUE EXPERIENCE SINCE YOUR LAST SESSION: (Complete this prior to today's session)

____

____

____

WRITE A SENTENCE ABOUT WHAT YOU REMEMBER FROM THE LAST SESSION: (Complete this prior to today's session)

____

____

____

KEY POINTS OR ISSUES COVERED TODAY:

____

____

____

HOMEWORK OR THINGS TO THINK ABOUT BETWEEN NOW AND MY NEXT SESSION:

____

____

____

HELPFULNESS OF SESSION IN HELPING TO RESOLVE ISSUES, PROBLEMS or MEET GOALS

(make a check on this scale):

Extremely Helpful—--------|-------------|------------|----------Not Helpful at all

10 5 1

SESSION NOTES or THOUGHTS

Weekly or Ongoing Therapy Sessions

SESSION DATE: ____________________PEOPLE PRESENT: ________________________

WRITE DOWN ANY CHANGE, EVENT, ISSUE EXPERIENCE SINCE YOUR LAST SESSION: (Complete this prior to today's session)

____

____

____

WRITE A SENTENCE ABOUT WHAT YOU REMEMBER FROM THE LAST SESSION: (Complete this prior to today's session)

____

____

____

KEY POINTS OR ISSUES COVERED TODAY:

____

____

____

HOMEWORK OR THINGS TO THINK ABOUT BETWEEN NOW AND MY NEXT SESSION:

____

____

____

HELPFULNESS OF SESSION IN HELPING TO RESOLVE ISSUES, PROBLEMS or MEET GOALS

(make a check on this scale):

Extremely Helpful———-------l-------------l------------l----------Not Helpful at all

10 5 1

SESSION NOTES or THOUGHTS

Weekly or Ongoing Therapy Sessions

SESSION DATE: ____________________PEOPLE PRESENT: ________________________

WRITE DOWN ANY CHANGE, EVENT, ISSUE EXPERIENCE SINCE YOUR LAST SESSION: (Complete this prior to today's session)

____

____

____

WRITE A SENTENCE ABOUT WHAT YOU REMEMBER FROM THE LAST SESSION: (Complete this prior to today's session)

____

____

____

KEY POINTS OR ISSUES COVERED TODAY:

____

____

____

HOMEWORK OR THINGS TO THINK ABOUT BETWEEN NOW AND MY NEXT SESSION:

____

____

____

HELPFULNESS OF SESSION IN HELPING TO RESOLVE ISSUES, PROBLEMS or MEET GOALS

(make a check on this scale):

Extremely Helpful——--------|-------------|------------|----------Not Helpful at all

10 5 1

SESSION NOTES or THOUGHTS

Weekly or Ongoing Therapy Sessions

SESSION DATE: ____________________PEOPLE PRESENT: ______________________

WRITE DOWN ANY CHANGE, EVENT, ISSUE EXPERIENCE SINCE YOUR LAST SESSION: (Complete this prior to today's session)

____

____

____

WRITE A SENTENCE ABOUT WHAT YOU REMEMBER FROM THE LAST SESSION: (Complete this prior to today's session)

____

____

____

KEY POINTS OR ISSUES COVERED TODAY:

____

____

____

HOMEWORK OR THINGS TO THINK ABOUT BETWEEN NOW AND MY NEXT SESSION:

____

____

____

HELPFULNESS OF SESSION IN HELPING TO RESOLVE ISSUES, PROBLEMS or MEET GOALS

(make a check on this scale):

Extremely Helpful———-------l-------------l------------l----------Not Helpful at all

10 5 1

SESSION NOTES or THOUGHTS

Weekly or Ongoing Therapy Sessions

SESSION DATE: ____________________PEOPLE PRESENT: ________________________

WRITE DOWN ANY CHANGE, EVENT, ISSUE EXPERIENCE SINCE YOUR LAST SESSION: (Complete this prior to today's session)

____

____

____

WRITE A SENTENCE ABOUT WHAT YOU REMEMBER FROM THE LAST SESSION: (Complete this prior to today's session)

____

____

____

KEY POINTS OR ISSUES COVERED TODAY:

____

____

____

HOMEWORK OR THINGS TO THINK ABOUT BETWEEN NOW AND MY NEXT SESSION:

____

____

____

HELPFULNESS OF SESSION IN HELPING TO RESOLVE ISSUES, PROBLEMS or MEET GOALS

(make a check on this scale):

Extremely Helpful—--------l-------------l------------l----------Not Helpful at all

10 5 1

SESSION NOTES or THOUGHTS

Weekly or Ongoing Therapy Sessions

SESSION DATE: ____________________PEOPLE PRESENT: ________________________

WRITE DOWN ANY CHANGE, EVENT, ISSUE EXPERIENCE SINCE YOUR LAST SESSION: (Complete this prior to today's session)

____

____

____

WRITE A SENTENCE ABOUT WHAT YOU REMEMBER FROM THE LAST SESSION: (Complete this prior to today's session)

____

____

____

KEY POINTS OR ISSUES COVERED TODAY:

____

____

____

HOMEWORK OR THINGS TO THINK ABOUT BETWEEN NOW AND MY NEXT SESSION:

____

____

____

HELPFULNESS OF SESSION IN HELPING TO RESOLVE ISSUES, PROBLEMS or MEET GOALS

(make a check on this scale):

Extremely Helpful—--------l-------------l------------l----------Not Helpful at all

10 5 1

SESSION NOTES or THOUGHTS

Weekly or Ongoing Therapy Sessions

SESSION DATE: ____________________PEOPLE PRESENT: ______________________

WRITE DOWN ANY CHANGE, EVENT, ISSUE EXPERIENCE SINCE YOUR LAST SESSION: (Complete this prior to today's session)

____

____

____

WRITE A SENTENCE ABOUT WHAT YOU REMEMBER FROM THE LAST SESSION: (Complete this prior to today's session)

____

____

____

KEY POINTS OR ISSUES COVERED TODAY:

____

____

____

HOMEWORK OR THINGS TO THINK ABOUT BETWEEN NOW AND MY NEXT SESSION:

____

____

____

HELPFULNESS OF SESSION IN HELPING TO RESOLVE ISSUES, PROBLEMS or MEET GOALS

(make a check on this scale):

Extremely Helpful—--------|-------------|------------|----------Not Helpful at all

10 5 1

SESSION NOTES or THOUGHTS

Weekly or Ongoing Therapy Sessions

SESSION DATE: ____________________PEOPLE PRESENT: ________________________

WRITE DOWN ANY CHANGE, EVENT, ISSUE EXPERIENCE SINCE YOUR LAST SESSION: (Complete this prior to today's session)

____

____

____

WRITE A SENTENCE ABOUT WHAT YOU REMEMBER FROM THE LAST SESSION: (Complete this prior to today's session)

____

____

____

KEY POINTS OR ISSUES COVERED TODAY:

____

____

____

HOMEWORK OR THINGS TO THINK ABOUT BETWEEN NOW AND MY NEXT SESSION:

____

____

____

HELPFULNESS OF SESSION IN HELPING TO RESOLVE ISSUES, PROBLEMS or MEET GOALS

(make a check on this scale):

Extremely Helpful—--------l-------------l------------l----------Not Helpful at all

10 5 1

SESSION NOTES or THOUGHTS

Weekly or Ongoing Therapy Sessions

SESSION DATE: ____________________PEOPLE PRESENT: ________________________

WRITE DOWN ANY CHANGE, EVENT, ISSUE EXPERIENCE SINCE YOUR LAST SESSION: (Complete this prior to today's session)

____

____

____

WRITE A SENTENCE ABOUT WHAT YOU REMEMBER FROM THE LAST SESSION: (Complete this prior to today's session)

____

____

____

KEY POINTS OR ISSUES COVERED TODAY:

____

____

____

HOMEWORK OR THINGS TO THINK ABOUT BETWEEN NOW AND MY NEXT SESSION:

____

____

____

HELPFULNESS OF SESSION IN HELPING TO RESOLVE ISSUES, PROBLEMS or MEET GOALS

(make a check on this scale):

Extremely Helpful——--------|-------------|------------|----------Not Helpful at all

10 5 1

SESSION NOTES or THOUGHTS

Weekly or Ongoing Therapy Sessions

SESSION DATE: ____________________PEOPLE PRESENT: ________________________

WRITE DOWN ANY CHANGE, EVENT, ISSUE EXPERIENCE SINCE YOUR LAST SESSION: (Complete this prior to today's session)

____

____

____

WRITE A SENTENCE ABOUT WHAT YOU REMEMBER FROM THE LAST SESSION: (Complete this prior to today's session)

____

____

____

KEY POINTS OR ISSUES COVERED TODAY:

____

____

____

HOMEWORK OR THINGS TO THINK ABOUT BETWEEN NOW AND MY NEXT SESSION:

____

____

____

HELPFULNESS OF SESSION IN HELPING TO RESOLVE ISSUES, PROBLEMS or MEET GOALS

(make a check on this scale):

Extremely Helpful—--------|-------------|------------|----------Not Helpful at all

10 5 1

SESSION NOTES or THOUGHTS

Weekly or Ongoing Therapy Sessions

SESSION DATE: ____________________ PEOPLE PRESENT: ______________________

WRITE DOWN ANY CHANGE, EVENT, ISSUE EXPERIENCE SINCE YOUR LAST SESSION: (Complete this prior to today's session)

____

____

____

WRITE A SENTENCE ABOUT WHAT YOU REMEMBER FROM THE LAST SESSION: (Complete this prior to today's session)

____

____

____

KEY POINTS OR ISSUES COVERED TODAY:

____

____

____

HOMEWORK OR THINGS TO THINK ABOUT BETWEEN NOW AND MY NEXT SESSION:

____

____

____

HELPFULNESS OF SESSION IN HELPING TO RESOLVE ISSUES, PROBLEMS or MEET GOALS

(make a check on this scale):

Extremely Helpful—--------|------------|-----------|----------Not Helpful at all

10 5 1

SESSION NOTES or THOUGHTS

Weekly or Ongoing Therapy Sessions

SESSION DATE: ____________________PEOPLE PRESENT: ______________________

WRITE DOWN ANY CHANGE, EVENT, ISSUE EXPERIENCE SINCE YOUR LAST SESSION: (Complete this prior to today's session)

____

____

____

WRITE A SENTENCE ABOUT WHAT YOU REMEMBER FROM THE LAST SESSION: (Complete this prior to today's session)

____

____

____

KEY POINTS OR ISSUES COVERED TODAY:

____

____

____

HOMEWORK OR THINGS TO THINK ABOUT BETWEEN NOW AND MY NEXT SESSION:

____

____

____

HELPFULNESS OF SESSION IN HELPING TO RESOLVE ISSUES, PROBLEMS or MEET GOALS

(make a check on this scale):

Extremely Helpful—--------l-------------l------------l----------Not Helpful at all

10 5 1

SESSION NOTES or THOUGHTS

Weekly or Ongoing Therapy Sessions

SESSION DATE: ____________________PEOPLE PRESENT: ______________________

WRITE DOWN ANY CHANGE, EVENT, ISSUE EXPERIENCE SINCE YOUR LAST SESSION: (Complete this prior to today's session)

____

____

____

WRITE A SENTENCE ABOUT WHAT YOU REMEMBER FROM THE LAST SESSION: (Complete this prior to today's session)

____

____

____

KEY POINTS OR ISSUES COVERED TODAY:

____

____

____

HOMEWORK OR THINGS TO THINK ABOUT BETWEEN NOW AND MY NEXT SESSION:

____

____

____

HELPFULNESS OF SESSION IN HELPING TO RESOLVE ISSUES, PROBLEMS or MEET GOALS

(make a check on this scale):

Extremely Helpful—--------l-------------l------------l----------Not Helpful at all

10 5 1

SESSION NOTES or THOUGHTS

Weekly or Ongoing Therapy Sessions

SESSION DATE: ____________________ PEOPLE PRESENT: ________________________

WRITE DOWN ANY CHANGE, EVENT, ISSUE EXPERIENCE SINCE YOUR LAST SESSION: (Complete this prior to today's session)

____

____

____

WRITE A SENTENCE ABOUT WHAT YOU REMEMBER FROM THE LAST SESSION: (Complete this prior to today's session)

____

____

____

KEY POINTS OR ISSUES COVERED TODAY:

____

____

____

HOMEWORK OR THINGS TO THINK ABOUT BETWEEN NOW AND MY NEXT SESSION:

____

____

____

HELPFULNESS OF SESSION IN HELPING TO RESOLVE ISSUES, PROBLEMS or MEET GOALS
(make a check on this scale):

Extremely Helpful—--------l-------------l------------l----------Not Helpful at all

10 5 1

SESSION NOTES or THOUGHTS

Weekly or Ongoing Therapy Sessions

SESSION DATE: ____________________PEOPLE PRESENT: ______________________

WRITE DOWN ANY CHANGE, EVENT, ISSUE EXPERIENCE SINCE YOUR LAST SESSION: (Complete this prior to today's session)

____

____

____

WRITE A SENTENCE ABOUT WHAT YOU REMEMBER FROM THE LAST SESSION: (Complete this prior to today's session)

____

____

____

KEY POINTS OR ISSUES COVERED TODAY:

____

____

____

HOMEWORK OR THINGS TO THINK ABOUT BETWEEN NOW AND MY NEXT SESSION:

____

____

____

HELPFULNESS OF SESSION IN HELPING TO RESOLVE ISSUES, PROBLEMS or MEET GOALS

(make a check on this scale):

Extremely Helpful—--------|------------|-----------|----------Not Helpful at all

10 5 1

SESSION NOTES or THOUGHTS

Weekly or Ongoing Therapy Sessions

SESSION DATE: ____________________PEOPLE PRESENT: ________________________

WRITE DOWN ANY CHANGE, EVENT, ISSUE EXPERIENCE SINCE YOUR LAST SESSION: (Complete this prior to today's session)

____

____

____

WRITE A SENTENCE ABOUT WHAT YOU REMEMBER FROM THE LAST SESSION: (Complete this prior to today's session)

____

____

____

KEY POINTS OR ISSUES COVERED TODAY:

____

____

____

HOMEWORK OR THINGS TO THINK ABOUT BETWEEN NOW AND MY NEXT SESSION:

____

____

____

HELPFULNESS OF SESSION IN HELPING TO RESOLVE ISSUES, PROBLEMS or MEET GOALS

(make a check on this scale):

Extremely Helpful—--------l-------------l------------l----------Not Helpful at all

10 5 1

SESSION NOTES or THOUGHTS

Weekly or Ongoing Therapy Sessions

SESSION DATE: ____________________ PEOPLE PRESENT: ______________________

WRITE DOWN ANY CHANGE, EVENT, ISSUE EXPERIENCE SINCE YOUR LAST SESSION: (Complete this prior to today's session)

____

____

____

WRITE A SENTENCE ABOUT WHAT YOU REMEMBER FROM THE LAST SESSION: (Complete this prior to today's session)

____

____

____

KEY POINTS OR ISSUES COVERED TODAY:

____

____

____

HOMEWORK OR THINGS TO THINK ABOUT BETWEEN NOW AND MY NEXT SESSION:

____

____

____

HELPFULNESS OF SESSION IN HELPING TO RESOLVE ISSUES, PROBLEMS or MEET GOALS

(make a check on this scale):

Extremely Helpful—---------|-------------|------------|----------Not Helpful at all

10 5 1

SESSION NOTES or THOUGHTS

Therapy/Counseling Ending Phase

PRESENT: ______________________________ Date: ____________________

To what extent were the original goals of your therapy met? Please Circle/Rate

6–Full Extent 5–Great 4–Some 3–Somewhat 2–Almost None 1–No Extent

Problem/Issue

Problem/Issue						
1.________________________	6	5	4	3	2	1
2.________________________	6	5	4	3	2	1
3.________________________	6	5	4	3	2	1

Looking back over your therapy experience, what ideas, suggestions, insights or homework assignments did you find most helpful to you?

____

____

____

What suggestions, if any, would you make to your therapist that could have improved his/her work with you?

____

____

____

In general, what was the most helpful aspect of your counseling/therapy experience?

____

____

____

Least helpful?

____

____

____

Therapy/Counseling Ending Phase (continued)

Overall Therapy Experience

6 5 4 3 2 1

Extremely Helpful Not At All

Rate the effectiveness of your therapist

6 5 4 3 2 1

Extremely Helpful Not At All

VII. Appendix

Psychotropic Medications

There is a chance that your psychotherapy experience will be augmented with the use of medication. If a person has an individual need and medical situation that could call for the use of medication, the therapist and client would discuss that option. If you and your therapist are in agreement about the use of medication, you will be referred to a healthcare provider who has prescription privileges if you are not receiving therapy from a psychiatrist or a nurse with prescription authority (in most cases, psychotherapists who are not psychiatrists [MD] or nurses do not have prescription authority). Those who have prescription privileges, and prescribe are called psychopharmacologist. A meeting with the psychopharmacologist will provide an assessment to help with choosing the right medication, dose and medication treatment plan.

Psychiatric medications, sometimes called psychotropic medications, do not cure the mental health disorder; rather, they treat the symptoms. The goal is for symptom relief, so a person can regain daily function. A number of people are reluctant to take any type of mental health medication due to the "side effects." Some individuals have significant reactions to even the smallest dosage of medication, while other individuals appear to show little to no reaction or side effects to even a megadose of a medication. There are many factors that impact a person's reaction to medication.

What follows is John Preston, PsyD's "Quick Reference to Psychotropic Medications." It covers most of the psychotropic medications typically used in treatment (psyc-fx.com). We like this list because it is divided into the different types of medications according to the illnesses they are usually treating. However, remember that a skilled psychopharmacologist may use mediation in one category to treat other types of mental health disorders. For example, a person who is manifesting a problem with anxiety may be prescribed an antidepressant, or an individual with a treatment-resistant depression may be advised to take a course of an antipsychotic. You can also check the National Institute of Mental Health Web site on Mental Health Medications (www.mimh.nih.gov/health/publications/mental-health-medications).

Psychotherapy and Homework

Researchers who have looked at the question of whether homework in psychotherapy helps have uniformly found that completing homework assignments for patients helped reduce symptom presentation. The link between homework use and positive psychotherapy outcome brought more relief to people experiencing affective disorders or problems with interpersonal relationships. We are offering several examples of homework exercises that the therapists use with their patients. In some cases, these exercises can be performed out of session. The therapist can elect to be a guide between the issue at hand and elements that the homework may be uncovering. Additionally, homework compliance may be viewed as an indicator of client commitment and involvement in psychotherapy. In any event, completing the homework has been found to be helpful in promoting work at hand in the psychotherapy relationship.

Examples

Frequently Encountered Psychotherapy Problems and Possible Homework Activities

Reason For Psychotherapy or Counseling: Couples Communication Improvement

Rational: Couples frequently say "our problem is with communication." Many never have learned how to talk to each other. Even their parents may not have known how to communicate for beneficial results. This is a systemic way of addressing this problem.

Homework: When a member of the couple realizes that they have a problem that involves their partner, they need to tell that person:

a. "I have a problem, and we need to talk."

b. The other person should acknowledge their partner has identified a problem and they need time to discuss the concern.

c. They decide if this is a good time for both parties or do they need to plan a time in the very near future? For example, this is not a good time if either party has been drinking or using any other mind-altering substance. Don't talk if the children may interrupt or you are about to leave for work, etc.

d. Once you have time, let the person who stated they have a problem state what they feel about the problem. Give the "problem stater" the floor without interrupting or defending yourself. They need to feel they have a place where they can safely tell what they think is their perception of an issue that is interfering with their sense of harmony in the relationship.

e. The "problem listener" must work at understanding the stator's perception so well that they can restate it with enough understanding to get the stater to say, "Okay, you get it!"

f. Together, you can explore solutions that you can both live with.

g. You try out a solution for a week, or whatever appears to be a reasonable time period.

h. Rediscuss the problem and see what happens.

NOTE: Never bring up a second issue at this time because the focus needs to be kept on the "problem stater's" issue or problem.

Top Three Stressors

Reason For Psychotherapy or Counseling: To help patients who are unable to prioritize their issues.

Rational: Sometimes patients come into therapy and don't know where to start. When this happens, think about what is causing the greatest amount of stress in your life.

Homework:

1. Write a list of all the things that are stressing you out. Think along these lines:

    - Relationships
    - Work
    - Money
    - Parents
    - Children
    - Future
    - Past

2. Rank order your list.

3. Pick the Top Three Stressors and discuss these with your therapist.

MAJOR DEPRESSION
RELAPS PREVENTION

It is natural to expect that relapse is a part of dealing with major depression. People who experience a "lifelong" history of depression are experiencing a chronic form of depression and the medical term for this type of depression is dysphoria.

Here are some things to help you deal with this type of depression:

- This disorder is most likely a biochemical problem and not reactive depression (e.g., reactive depressions are typically reactions to a loss, such as the death of a close family member or friend, or the breakup of a marriage).
- If you have been treated with medication in the past, you might be wise to check in with your prescriber.
- Think about your life more positively.
- Regulate your emotions more effectively and behave more adaptively.
- Schedule posttherapy "booster" sessions.

Write out a Relapse Prevention Plan that includes:

- How you will recognize when you are getting depressed again.
- Who you can call for support.
- What you can do to make yourself feel better.

Reason For Psychotherapy or Counseling: Understanding Martial Conflict and/or Issues: "My Partner's List"

Rational: Even though we think we know our spouses or partners it is surprising how we don't really understand and in some cases can't even identify the issues they have with us.

Homework:

- List the top concerns that *your partner* would say they have with you.
- In the next session you read off the concerns you came up with and see if your partner agrees with the list of concerns.
- Cross off your list any you were not right about, correct any that you did not have exactly right and add to your list any issues you may have missed.

Automatic Thinking

Rational: Some people will see, or hear, something and will automatically have a negative thought. Cognitive psychologists refer to this, when in extreme, as cognitive distortion. An example would be a student who receives a bad grade and states, "I am the dumbest kid in the school, and this proves it." We want the people we work with to gain a more balanced view of themselves.

Homework:

- Identify some negative automatic (sometimes called irrational) thoughts about a problem.
- What feelings do you get when you have these thoughts?
- What would be a more reasonable thought for that problem?

Example:

Problem…

1. I'm calling this woman from work who I would like to ask out on a date.
2. I started calling on Friday and have left two messages!
3. She has not returned my call.

Automatic thoughts…

a. She must see my name on the caller ID and is not interested, or doesn't even want to talk to me.

b. No one would ever want to date me.

Feelings…

Depressed and frustrated

Rational thoughts…

a. Maybe she doesn't remember or recognize my name. We do work in two different departments.

b. Maybe she hasn't been home all weekend and hasn't checked her voice mail.

Reason For Psychotherapy or Counseling: "What gets in my way?"

Rational: We all have something, maybe many things, that get in our way. Whatever the thing or issue that gets in your way, it needs to be identified. It helps to label the problem and externalize it from our self. Viewing ourselves and the problem one and the same is *not* helpful.

Homework: Write a description of your problem(s):

____

____

____

____

____

____

____

____

Name the problem(s):

________________________ ________________________

________________________ ________________________

________________________ ________________________

________________________ ________________________

________________________ ________________________

________________________ ________________________

For each problem, state things you have done, or could do, to overcome the problem:

____

____

____

____

____

____

____

____

Have a discussion with your therapist about your next steps.

Reference

Goleman, D (1995), Emotional Intelligence, Bantam Dell, New York, NY

Mayer, J.D. and Salovey, P. (1997), "What is Emotional Intelligence? In P. Salovey and D. Sluyer (Eds) Emotional Development and Emotional Intelligence: Implications for educators (pp 3-31). New York: BASIC

Preston, J. (2014). Quick Drug Reference Guide. Retrieved from http://psyd-fx.com/wp-content/uploads/2014/06/Quick-Reference-2014Proof_Page_2.jpg

CPSIA information can be obtained
at www.ICGtesting.com
Printed in the USA
FFOW01n1826160116
20485FF

9 781478 739067